Top Dogs

I Love My German Shepherd

Abigail Beal

PowerKiDS press

New York

This book is dedicated to you and your pet— a special friendship based on loyalty, respect, and kindness.

Published in 2011 by The Rosen Publishing Group, Inc.
29 East 21st Street, New York, NY 10010

First Edition

Editor: Joanne Randolph
Book Design: Greg Tucker

Photo Credits: Cover, pp. 5, 7, 8, 9, 10 (left), 10–11 (main), 11 (right), 12, 13, 16, 17, 20–21, 22 Shutterstock.com; p. 4 Victoria Yee/Getty Images; p. 6 Popperfoto/Getty Images; p. 14 © Olivier Digoit/Peter Arnold, Inc.; p. 15 Brian Stevenson/Getty Images; p. 18 Jeff Topping/AFP/Getty Images; p. 19 iStockphoto/Thinkstock.

Library of Congress Cataloging-in-Publication Data

Beal, Abigail.
I love my German shepherd / by Abigail Beal. — 1st ed.
    p. cm. — (Top dogs)
Includes index.
ISBN 978-1-4488-2535-6 (library binding) — ISBN 978-1-4488-2654-4 (pbk.) —
ISBN 978-1-4488-2655-1 (6-pack)
1. German shepherd dog—Juvenile literature. I. Title.
SF429.G37B43 2011
636.737'6—dc22
                              2010020811

Manufactured in the United States of America

CPSIA Compliance Information: Batch #WW11PK: For Further Information contact Rosen Publishing, New York, New York at 1-800-237-9932

Contents

Meet the German Shepherd

It is said that a dog is man's best friend. There is no better way to describe a German shepherd. Ask anyone who owns one of these dogs. He will likely tell you how much he loves his German shepherd.

As a puppy, your German shepherd will need you to guide it patiently. This is true of any new puppy. German

German shepherds are loyal. This means they will always be by your side. Take good care of your German shepherd, and it will live a long, healthy life with you.

shepherds are very smart, and they enjoy learning commands. German shepherds are so easy to train that they are often used to do important jobs. These jobs include helping the police or working as **service dogs**. These things also make the German shepherd a great family pet.

German shepherds have long, pointed noses and pointed ears that stand up on their heads.

German Shepherd History

German shepherds were first used to guard sheep in the German countryside. In the beginning any dog used to guard animals in Germany was called a German shepherd. There were no rules in place about how this dog should look or act.

In 1891, the Phylax Society began to **standardize** sheep-herding dogs. This means they worked to **breed** dogs

After World War I, U.S. soldiers brought home German shepherd puppies. They talked about how brave and loyal this breed had been during their wartime service.

to have a **consistent** appearance and character. In 1899, Max Emil Friedrich von Stephanitz went to a herding-dog show. There he saw a German shepherd that had all the features that owners valued in the breed. He bought the dog and used it to set the breed standard.

The breed standard says the German shepherd's body should be longer than it is tall. It should move with great power as well.

What Does a German Shepherd Look Like?

German shepherds are known for their wolflike looks. German shepherds can be almost any color. However, the most common colors are black and tan and black and red.

This dog has pointed ears that are always listening for commands or signs of danger. The German shepherd has dark,

This German shepherd is black with tan fur in a few small spots. Some German shepherds have longer fur on the sides of their faces and necks, as this one does.

almond-shaped eyes. Its sharp eyesight serves it well as a working dog and as a **protective** family pet.

A German shepherd is a large, solid, and strong dog. It can weigh between 75 and 95 pounds (34–43 kg) and stand 26 inches (66 cm) tall at its shoulder. Even when at rest, this dog can quickly respond to commands.

Always Ready

Some people think the German shepherd is an unfriendly dog, but this is not true. This dog is protective of its family and naturally cautious of strangers, though. However, if German shepherds have been **socialized** the right way, they should let

German shepherds can make great playmates for other dogs if they are introduced to them at a young age.

strangers come up to them without becoming **aggressive**. German shepherds are very **loyal** and trust their owner's commands. It is important to treat your dog with respect and kindness.

The German shepherd needs a lot of exercise. German shepherds are known for being quick and full of energy. They will always be ready to go for a walk or to play.

Confident, Brave, and Useful

German shepherds are **confident** and brave dogs. This leads many people to pick the large and strong German shepherd to protect their families. This is also what leads people to use these dogs for police or military work. German shepherds tend to stay calm even when there is a lot going on around them. This feature helps these dogs do many jobs well.

Here a police officer and his German shepherd get ready for some training. This breed bonds strongly to its owner, which is what makes them such great working dogs!

German shepherds are known for their **intelligence**. These dogs enjoy being useful and are quick to serve their owners. Like any dog, though, German shepherds need socialization and training. These things will help them become better family pets.

Are you ready for a workout? This German shepherd is training for its job as a police dog. German shepherds love to work!

Caring for Your Pet

Owning a dog is a big job. Your German shepherd counts on you for good care. It is important to give German shepherds clean water and healthy food. They may also enjoy treats, but too many snacks can be unhealthy for your pet.

Giving it healthy foods is just one part of pet care. German shepherds need regular brushing, exercise, and training.

Pet owners should brush their German shepherds once or twice a week. This keeps them from shedding their fur all over the couch!

Giving your German shepherd **identification** tags and a collar lets others know this dog is yours. Today microchipping also helps identify dogs that get lost. Ask your veterinarian about other ways you can help your German shepherd live a long, healthy life.

German shepherds are happy to walk or run with their owners. Just as exercise is healthy for people, it is healthy for our pets, too.

Training Your Pet

German shepherds are smart and want to please their owners. You can start training your dog as a puppy. It is important to be consistent with training. **Praise** your German shepherd when it does something you like. Ignore your pet when it does something you do not like or gently show your dog the right things to do.

German shepherd puppies want to make their owners happy, they just need to learn the rules. This German shepherd puppy is learning how to sit on command.

Introduce your dog to other animals, children, and new things. It is one of the most important things you can do for your dog.

You will want to teach your German shepherd some basic commands. These include teaching your pet to sit and stay when you ask it to do so. You could also teach your dog more **advanced** tricks or games. You can go beyond the basics with your smart new pet!

German Shepherds at Work

While many people first think of the German shepherd as a great pet, this fine dog is also a hard worker. Over the years, German shepherds have been called upon to do many different jobs.

Since World War I, German shepherds have been military dogs. During wartime, they rescue soldiers, find mines, and carry food and

This German shepherd is working as a service dog for someone who cannot see. Service dogs go though a lot of training to do their work.

drugs. They often work as police dogs, too. German shepherds also make wonderful service dogs. You have likely seen German shepherds guiding the blind or helping people with disabilities live more independently. German shepherds are great dogs!

German shepherds are also used by search and rescue teams. Their sharp senses make them just right for this job.

RESCUE

Is a German Shepherd Right for You?

The German shepherd is the right dog for many people. Owners like this dog for its loyalty, intelligence, and trainability. These dogs can make wonderful family pets and good friends. It is important that you show your German shepherd good friendship in return.

German shepherds need regular walks and lots of playtime. Do not pick a German shepherd if you will be too busy to walk it. This is unfair to your pet and can also lead to

German shepherds are strong and active, but they are also happy sitting by your side as you watch TV or read a book. Is a German shepherd the right dog for you?

problems. Your dog needs consistent rules and a routine on which it can count. If you can do these things, you will have a great pet!

German Shepherd Facts

1. Rin Tin Tin was an American Red Cross dog during World War I. Rin Tin Tin appeared in 26 films for Warner Brothers and received 10,000 fan letters weekly.

2. Rin Tin Tin II and Rin Tin Tin IV both appeared in the TV show called *The Adventures of Rin Tin Tin*.

3. The full name for this breed is German shepherd dog, but most people just call the dogs German shepherds.

4. The first German shepherds were trained for police work around 1900 in Ghent, Belgium.

5. The first German shepherd to work as a guide dog was named Buddy. He started working in 1928.

6. Some famous people have owned German shepherds. Roy Rogers had one named Bullet. Jacqueline Kennedy's German shepherd was named Clipper, and Franklin Delano Roosevelt had one named Major.

Glossary

advanced (ad-VANTSD) Harder or needing more skill.

aggressive (uh-GREH-siv) Being quick to fight.

breed (BREED) To bring a male and a female animal together so they will have babies.

confident (KON-fih-dent) Having a firm belief in oneself and one's abilities.

consistent (kun-SIS-tent) Stays the same.

identification (eye-den-tuh-fuh-KAY-shun) Something that tells what something is.

intelligence (in-TEH-luh-jents) Smartness.

loyal (LOY-ul) Faithful to a person or an idea.

praise (PRAYZ) To say nice things about someone or something.

protective (pruh-TEK-tiv) Having to do with keeping something or someone from being hurt.

service dogs (SIR-vis DAWGZ) Dogs that do jobs for people.

socialized (SOH-shuh-lyzd) Made ready to be around others.

standardize (STAN-dur-dyz) To make like others in a group.

Index

Web Sites

Due to the changing nature of Internet links, PowerKids Press has developed an online list of Web sites related to the subject of this book. This site is updated regularly. Please use this link to access the list:
www.powerkidslinks.com/topd/germshep/